Short Surahs

WORKBOOK

Elementary Level   ∞   Qur'anic Studies

by Hajjah Noura Durkee

IQRA'
International Educational Foundation

Part of a Comprehensive and Systematic Program of Islamic Studies

A Workbook for Qur'a'nic Studies
Elementary Level

Short Surahs, Workbook

Chief Program Editors:
Dr. Abidullah al-Ansari Ghazi
(Ph.D. History of Religion,
Harvard University)

Dr. Tasneema Khatoon Ghazi
(Ph.D. Curriculum and Reading,
University of Minnesota)

Reviewers
Dr. Tasneema Khatoon Ghazi
(Ph.D. Curriculum and Reading,
University of Minnesota)

Fadel Abdallah
(M.A. Arabic Islamic Studies,
University of Minnesota)

Language Editing:
Fadel Abdallah
(M.A. Arabic Islamic Studies,
University of Minnesota)

Arabic Typesetting:
Randa Zaiter

Design:
Jennifer Mazzoni
(B.A. Illustration,
Columbia College, Chicago)

Fourth Printing September, 2007
Fifth Printing December, 2009
Sixth Printing June, 2012
Seventh Printing March, 2015
Eigth Printing March, 2016
Ninth Printing April, 2017
Printed in India

IQRA' International Educational Foundation
7450 Skokie Blvd., Skokie, IL 60077
Tel: 847-673-4072, Fax: 847-673-4095
Website: www.iqrafoundation.com

Library of Congress Control Number: **2013902797**
ISBN # **1-56316-103-6**

Table of Contents

IQRA's Note

This workbook is written with the purpose of providing meaningful and interesting reinforcement to the children after they have finished reading a chapter in the textbook. Exercises are developed with the intentions of helping the students in grasping the main ideas, memorizing the basic facts, and comprehending the issues presented in the text. Furthermore, through these exercises an attempt has been made to enhance students' abilities in problem solving, sequencing, drawing inferences, evaluating, analyzing and synthesizing.

Each exercise corresponds to a lesson in the textbook. In order to benefit from the exercises, the teacher should read through the corresponding lesson in the textbook with the class and then ask the students to work on the exercise in the workbook.

The exercises provided in the workbook are developed with an understanding of the abilities and interests of 7 to 9 year olds.

It will be helpful to follow these strategies while teaching in the class:

Introducing the Lesson: Read each lesson in the textbook with the children in the class.

Introducing the Vocabulary: Discuss the meaning of each new word encountered in the lesson.

Reading and Reflection: Ask the children to read the lesson again silently to themselves and to think about the specific issues dealt with in the lesson.

Asking Comprehension Questions: After the children have read the lesson, ask questions (literal, inferential and critical) about the contents of the chapter.

Providing Practice: Open the same lesson in the workbook and discuss the relevant exercise with the class. Help the students with the first problem, then ask them to work on the remaining exercises themselves.

Providing Feedback: Always remember to look at the completed exercise and comment on the work. It is necessary for motivation. Rewarding good work encourages the children to do quality work.

LESSON 1   *Al-Fātiḥah*

The Opening

Read pages 4 and 5 in your textbook and fill in the blanks:

1. *Sūrah-al-Fātiḥah* is known as the " _____ of the Book."

2. We recite this *sūrah* at the beginning of each _____ in our *ṣalāh*.

3. _____ alone is Master of the Day of _____ .

4. Allah's (﷽) path is _____ , not crooked.

5. The _____ wants to get us off Allah's ﷽ path.

6. *Sūrah-al-Fātiḥah* is the _____ *sūrah* of the Qur'ān.

7. Two beautiful Names of Allah ﷽ at the beginning of this *sūrah* are:

   _____ and _____ .

8. Allah ﷽ is the Lord of <u>all</u> the _____ .

Answer the following, choosing the right words from the list:

Prophets	Master	martyrs	praise	truthful people
first verse	Lord	day	second	seven	Most Merciful

1. What kinds of people follow the path of Islam?

   _____ , _____ , _____ .

2. How many verses are in *Sūrat-al-Fātiḥah* ? _____

3. What is the meaning of *al-ḥamd* ? _____

4. What is the translation of يَوْم ? _____

5. Which verse says, "Praise be to Allah, Lord of the Worlds"? _____

6. Three words in the *sūrah* which describe Allah ﷻ:

   _____ , _____ , _____ .

Answer the following, choosing the right words from the list:

1. What is the meaning of :

   ؟ بِسْمِ ٱللَّهِ ٱلرَّحْمٰنِ ٱلرَّحِيْمِ

   _____

   _____

2. Draw pictures of four things that people worship or have worshipped as idols besides Allah ﷻ.

A _____

B _____

C _____

D _____

3. Can any of these things help us as Allah ﷻ can help us?

(circle one) :   yes   no

4. What is a path?

_____

_____

5. Muslims say *al-Fātiḥah* for many reasons besides the *ṣalāh*. We say it when we begin something new, when we ask Allah ﷻ to bless somebody, when we feel worried or afraid, when we want safety, when we want to thank Allah ﷻ. Can you describe some time when **you** might want to recite *al-Fātiḥah?*

_____

_____

_____

_____

_____

LESSON 2:

An-Nās

The People

Read page 14, Lesson 2 of the textbook, and fill in the blanks:

1. *Sūrah an-Nās* is the _____ *sūrah* of the Qur'ān.

2. We should say this *sūrah* when we _____ and also in the

   _____ .

3. Ugly thoughts sometimes appear in our _____ .

4. Both _____ and people can be good or _____ .

5. There are _____ *sūrahs* in the Qur'ān.

6. In this *sūrah,* we ask Allah ﷻ to protect us from _____ .

Answer the following questions, follow any given instructions:

1. This is a *sūrah* about everyone. *Nās* is sometimes translated as *man,* sometimes as *mankind,* sometimes as *people,* sometimes as *humankind.* Write the names of some of the people or kinds of people you know: (ex: woman, mother, boy, girl, friend, teacher).

   _____

   _____

   _____

2. There are many words in this *sūrah* that describe Allah ﷻ. Can you write some of them?

_____ , _____ , _____

_____ , _____

3. *Shaiṭān* whispers to all of us. Describe a time when *Shaiṭān* whispered to you. What did you do about it?

_____

_____

_____

_____

4. Look at lesson 2 in your textbook and write the meanings of these words in English:

A. قُلْ *Qul* _____

B. رَبّ *Rabb* _____

C. مَلِكِ *maliki* _____

D. مِنْ *min* _____

E. وَ *wa* _____

F. يُوَسْوِسُ *yuwaswisu* _____

G. صُدُوْرْ *ṣudūr* _____

H. فِى *fī* _____

5. Here is a picture of your heart. Write inside it five good feelings you want to keep in it, and outside it five bad feelings you will try to keep outside: (Below is a list of words you can choose from. You may add to the list.)

'Imān, happy, angry, mean, loving, contented, hopeful, open, cruel, sneaky, suspicious, warm, tender, selfish, bitter, sour, friendly, sweet, hateful

LESSON 3 *Al- Falaq*

Daybreak

1. In *Sūrah al-Falaq* and in *Sūrah an-Nās* we say:
   a' ūdhu bi Rabbi : I take refuge in the Lord

   To take refuge means to hide in, to find safety with, to be protected in. Do you have a favorite hiding place? Or do you have someone you always go to when you are hurt or scared? Can you make a picture here of that hiding place or the person you go to?

2. *Falaq,* in Arabic, means the crack of dawn. It is the very first light that shows the sun will soon be rising. After *falaq,* the night begins to go away. We know Allah ﷻ is bringing us light, and we ask His protection from:

A. The _____ of _____ as it spreads.

B. The _____ of _____ who blow on knots (black magicians).

C. The _____ of _____ when he shows jealousy.

3. We also ask protection from the "mischief of created things." Mischief means being bad, causing trouble or harm. Can you think of three ways Allah's ﷻ creation could cause mischief to you? (Example: a dog could bite you, or a stone could fall on your head.)

A. _____

_____

B. _____

_____

C. _____

_____

4. How do jealous people feel?
   Color the words that describe jealousy **red,** and the others **blue:**

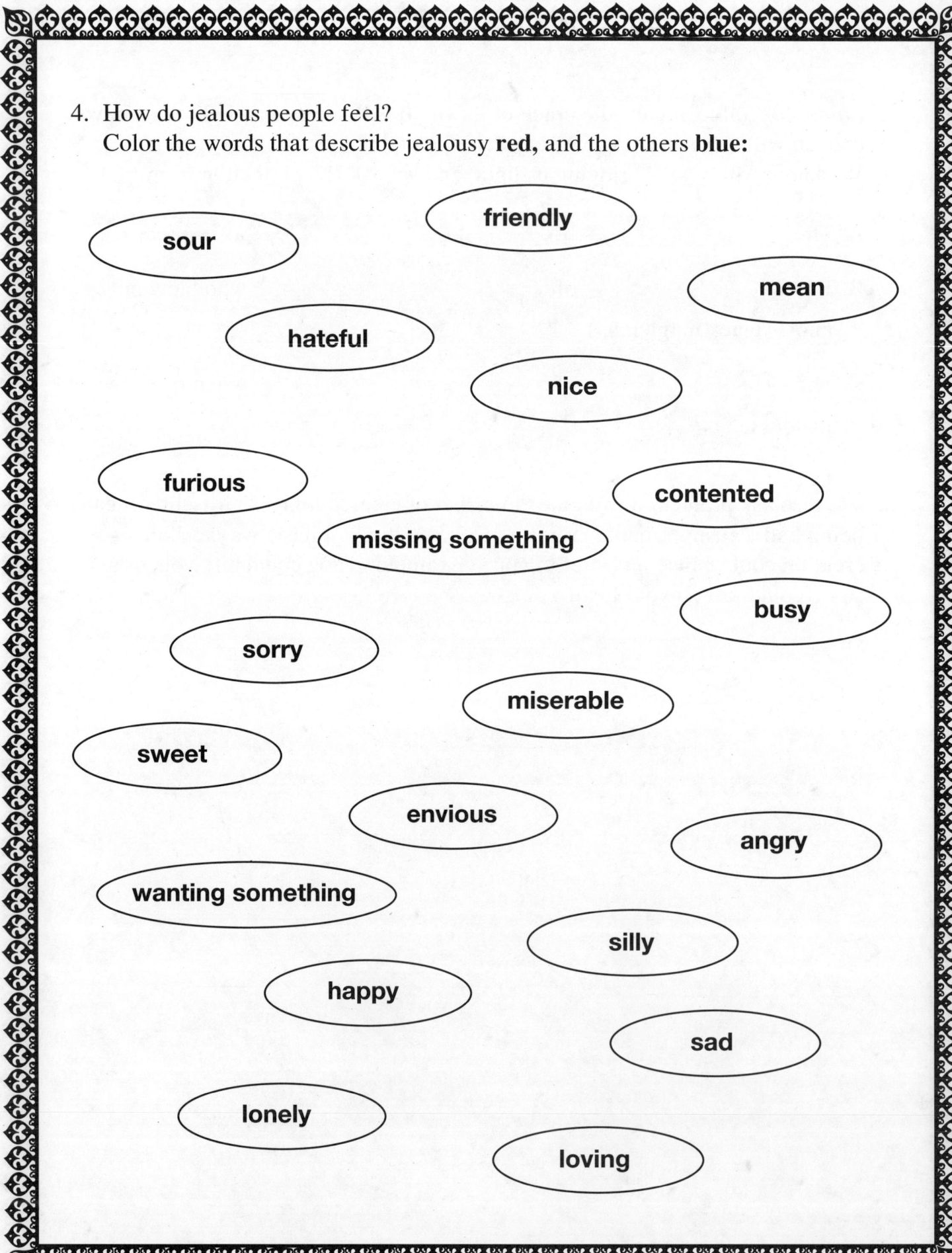

friendly

sour

mean

hateful

nice

furious

contented

missing something

busy

sorry

miserable

sweet

envious

angry

wanting something

silly

happy

sad

lonely

loving

5. Allah ﷻ is the Creator of everything. List as many different creations of His as you can think of in five minutes.

1. _____
2. _____
3. _____
4. _____
5. _____
6. _____
7. _____
8. _____
9. _____
10. _____

11. _____
12. _____
13. _____
14. _____
15. _____
16. _____
17. _____
18. _____
19. _____
20. _____

....more?

6. What do these words mean?

A. شَرّ *sharr* _____

B. أَعُوذُ *'a'ūdhu* _____

C. مِنْ *min* _____
   (review)

D. قُلْ *qul* _____
   (review)

E. غَاسِقْ *ghāsiq* _____

Sincerity

1. How many gods do you worship? (circle one of these)

1   5   99   360

2. What is the meaning of *Tawḥīd*? _____

Here is a "Word Ring." Find these words and circle them:

| *tawḥīd* one birth equal name lamb be mean idol angel |

There are more words *inside* of words. How many can you find?

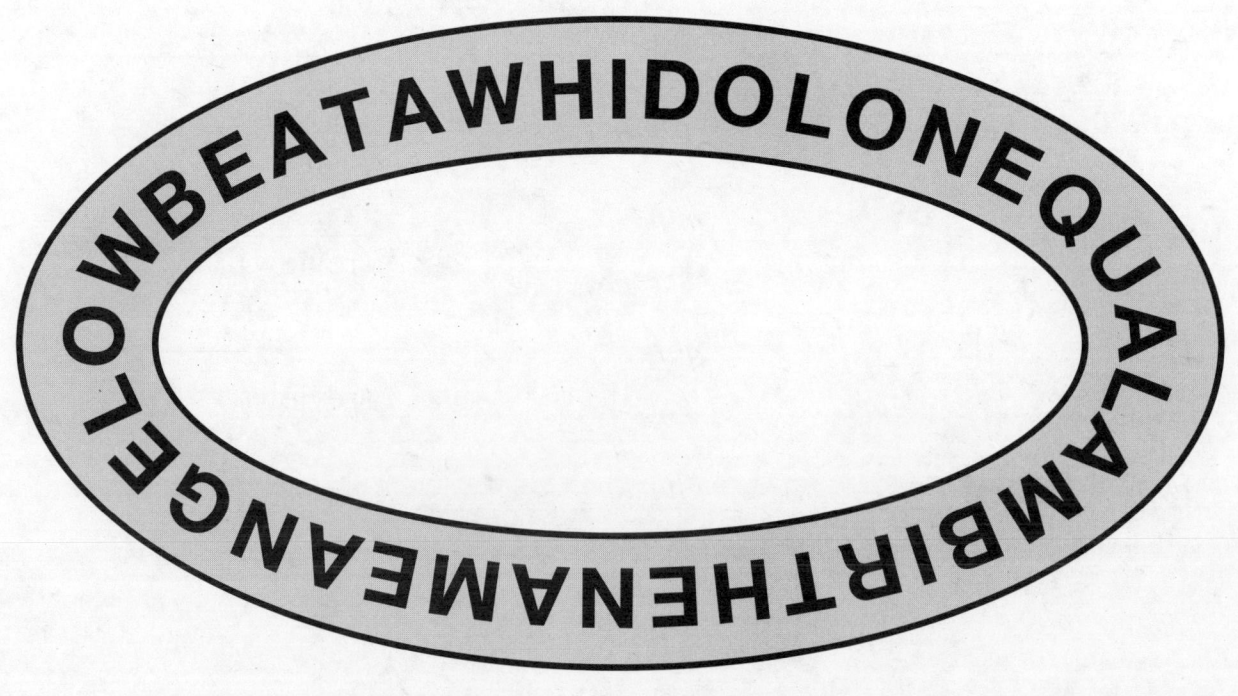

Check 'true' or 'false':   true   false

1. Allah ﷻ has a mother.   _____   _____

2. Allah ﷻ has no children.   _____   _____

3. Allah ﷻ has only one son.   _____   _____

4. Allah ﷻ can die.   _____   _____

5. Allah ﷻ is two.   _____   _____

6. Allah ﷻ is forever.   _____   _____

7. Allah ﷻ is like us.   _____   _____

8. Allah ﷻ has a father.   _____   _____

9. Allah ﷻ created us.   _____   _____

10. Allah ﷻ protects us.   _____   _____

11. Allah ﷻ made the earth.   _____   _____

12. Allah ﷻ did not make the animals.   _____   _____

13. Allah ﷻ loves us.   _____   _____

14. Allah ﷻ makes the rain.   _____   _____

15. Allah ﷻ cannot make miracles.   _____   _____

Answer the following questions. Follow any given instructions:

1. There are lots of stars but only one sun. There are lots of people but only one mother gave birth to you. Can you think of more things that are single, only one? _____

    _____

    _____

    Can you draw one of them?

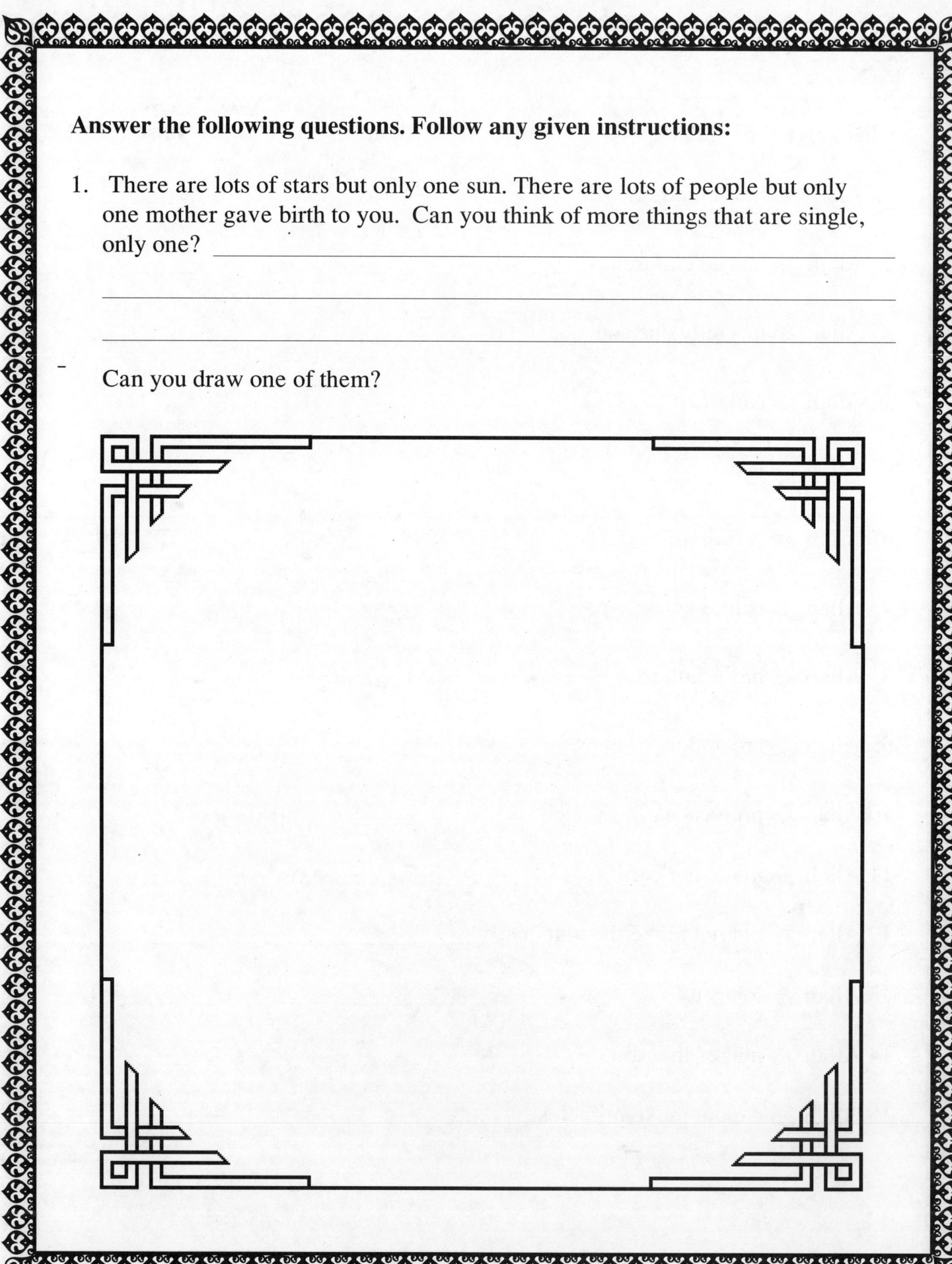

2. In *Sūrat al-'Ikhlāṣ* there are some words that say what Allah ﷻ is, and some words that describe what Allah ﷻ is not. Put them in these two columns:

IS

IS NOT (or does not)

_____   _____
_____   _____
_____   _____
_____   _____
_____   _____
_____   _____
_____   _____
_____   _____

3. COLOR ... Allah is:

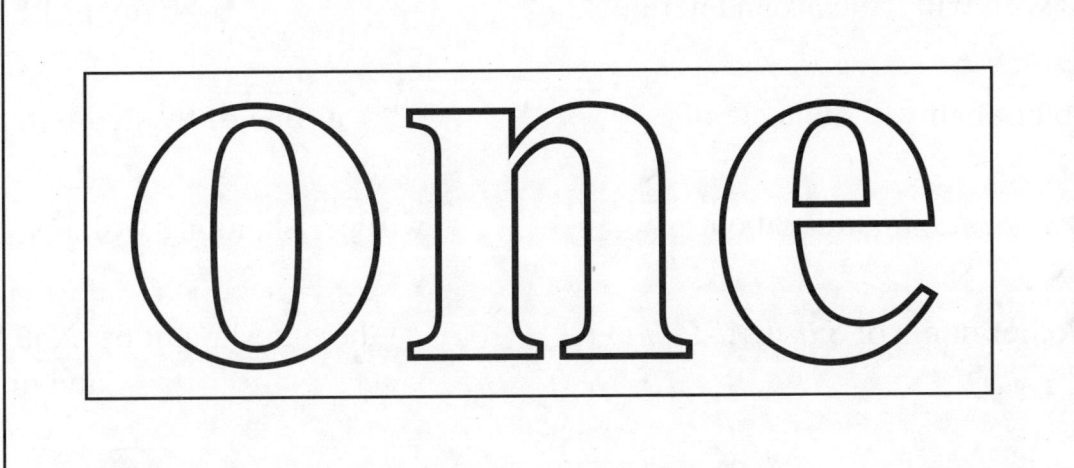

The Flame

Match the first part of the sentence to the second; follow the example given with number 1:

1. In time of danger   Rasūlullāh ﷺ

2. 'Abū Lahab and his wife   put thorns in the path of Rasulullah ﷺ

3. The Makkans knew Muḥammad ﷺ   *Al-Masad.*

4. The wife of 'Abū Lahab   people climbed the mount of Ṣafa.

5. "'Abū Lahab" means   were the enemies of Rasūlullāh ﷺ.

6. The hands and power of 'Abū Lahab   was honest and trustworthy.

7. His wife will have around her neck   "Father of Flame."

8. 'Abū Lahab was an uncle of   a rope of twisted palm fiber.

9. *Surah Al-Lahab* talks about   will perish, along with his wealth.

10. Another name of *Sūrah Al-Lahab* is   the punishment of 'Abū Lahab and his wife.

Choose the best words to complete the sentences:

people father punishment flames idol lies enemies thorns Al-'Uzzā

1. This *surah* talks about the _____ of 'Abū Lahab and his wife.

2. They were great _____ of Islam and the Prophet ﷺ.

3. "'Abū" means _____ . 'Abū Lahab means _____

   _____ .

4. 'Abū Lahab worshipped an _____ named _____ .

5. 'Abū Lahab's wife put _____ in the Prophet's ﷺ path and also

   told _____ to turn people away from him.

Circle the word that does not belong with the others:

1. neck   hands   flame   feet

2. 'Ali ؓ   'Abū Lahab   'Umar ؓ   'Abū Bakr ؓ

3. Makkah   Madīnah   Chicago   Al-Quds

4. protection   safety   fear   refuge

5. permission   acceptance   punishment   approval

People in Makkah called Rasūlullāh ﷺ *Al-'Amīn,* "The Trustworthy." Circle the words that mean a person can be trusted.

cheat

a liar

untrustworthy

truthful

unfaithful

noble

sneaky

reliable

just

fair

tricky

unjust

unfair

honest

straight

Here is a story about 'Abū Lahab. Read it and answer the questions:

The Muslims defeated the *Quraish* at the Battle of *Badr,* and many Makkans were killed. When this news came to Makkah, 'Abū Lahab was sitting in a large tent by the Ka'bah. With him was his sister-in-law, 'Umm al-Faḍl, and a slave named 'Abū Rafi'. The slave, secretly a Muslim, was so happy and excited that he shouted. 'Abū Lahab was a big fat man and had a fiery temper. He became so angry that he hit the slave, sat on him and kept pounding him. 'Umm al-Faḍl, who was a secret Muslim also, picked up a wooden pole and hit 'Abū Lahab hard on the head with it, because he was being unjust and unfair. From this wound he got very sick, had a high fever, and died.

1. Was 'Abū Lahab a fair and just man? _____

2. From this story, how would you describe 'Abū Lahab? _____

   _____

   _____

   _____

   _____

3. From the beginning, Islam helped people who were weak and were pushed around by others. What kinds of people do you think they were? _____

   _____

   _____

   _____

4. 'Abū Lahab had been one of the richest and most powerful men in Makkah. This *sūrah* says that his wealth will not be of any use to him. What do you think this means? _____

_____

_____

_____

Write the correct English words from your vocabulary lists:

1. يَدَآ   *yadā*   _____

2. مَالُهُ   *māluhū*   (his) _____

3. نَارًا   *nāran*   _____

4. جِيدِهَا   *jīdi-hā*   (her) _____

5. حَبْل   *ḥabl*   _____

6. لَهَبْ   *lahab*   _____

7. مَّسَد   *masad*   _____

   (review)

Victory

Read this paragraph, then answer the questions:

In the early days of Islam, the Muslims were few and weak. The *Kuffār* hurt them, beat them, and made their lives very difficult. However, the Muslims remained determined and full of faith. Allah ﷻ helped them and slowly strengthened them with knowledge and stronger faith inside, and more people and wealth outside. At last, the Muslims conquered Makkah and all the rest of Arabia, and all the tribes embraced Islam. The Muslims were very happy about this. They were also very merciful to the people who had hurt them before. They did not kill or torment them. They were polite to them and let them go in peace. When the Muslims won the victory, they made it easy for all to become Muslims, and be members of the *'Ummah*.

Underline the correct answer:

1. The Muslims hurt the *kuffār* and killed them.
   The Muslims were merciful to the *kuffār*.
   The Muslims were afraid of the *kuffār*.

2. The *kuffār* went on fighting the Muslims.
   The *kuffār* all embraced Islam.
   The *kuffār* were all killed.

3. The Muslims had always been strong.
   The Muslims had become strong slowly.
   The Muslims had always been weak.

Answer the following questions. Follow any given instructions:

1. The nature of Islam is mercy. Allah ﷻ calls Himself the Most Merciful and the Giver of Mercy. The Prophet ﷺ, was the most merciful of people. Put an X by the sentences you think are true about mercy.

   A. _____ A merciful person likes to help.

   B. _____ A merciful person never kills anyone, even in battle or self defense.

   C. _____ A merciful person gives out quick, clear punishments.

   D. _____ A merciful person likes to forgive.

   E. _____ A merciful person tries to understand the other's point of view.

   F. _____ A merciful person always wants to get his or her own way.

   G. _____ A merciful person takes revenge and likes it.

   H. _____ A merciful person doesn't show off when he or she wins.

   I. _____ A merciful person knows that Allah ﷻ cares for every living creature.

2. Allah ﷻ is ready to turn towards us and to forgive us if we turn towards Him and ask for forgiveness. This turning is called *"tawbah."* Can you write three sentences about times you might want to turn towards Allah ﷻ and hope He will send His Mercy on you?

   A. _____

   B. _____

   C. _____

3. Here's a crossword puzzle; fill in the words from the list provided.

surah, book, easy, off, at, qul, universes, ha, nabi, need, patient, brave, safe, shaitan, up, ma, Allah, generous, are, so, hamd, love, on, small, salah, by, dawn, deer, go, al, open,

down:
1. an Arabic word for prophet
2. able to wait
3. to move from here to there
4. the Name of God
5. secure, not dangerous
6. opposite of 'large'
7. something to read
8. to have a use for
9. an animal, sounds just like 'dear'
10. to be, plural
11. not difficult
12. rhymes with 'go'
13. not 'on'
14. 'what' in Arabic
15. opposite of 'down'
16. 'praise' in Arabic
17. the devil
18. 'say' in Arabic

across:
19. all the worlds
20. having a lot of courage
3. likes to give
4. 'the' in Arabic
21. What Muslims do five times a day (pray)
22. the sound of a small laugh
7. beside, next to
23. not 'off'
9. earliest morning
10. last two letters of 'cat'
24. a feeling of caring
12. a chapter of the Qur'ān (Arabic)
25. not shut

LESSON 7

Al-Kāfirūn

The Disbelievers

Answer the following questions. Follow any given instructions:

1. Underline the right word:

    A. Islam is the   **only / tenth**   dīn of Allah ﷻ.

    B. We should   **force / invite**   our neighbors to believe in Allah ﷻ and
       His prophets.

    C. The word '*Al-Kāfirūn*' means   **the Quraish / the Disbelievers.**

    D. A Muslim   **can worship / cannot worship**   what the *Kuffār* worship.

    E. If a non-Muslim decides to become Muslim, we   **turn him/her away
       / welcome him/her.**

2. This *sūrah, Al-Kāfirūn,* has forms of the words 'worship' or 'worshippers' in
    it many times. The 'root,' or base of this word is 'a - ba - da. Write this word
    and try to learn it in its English sound:

    ## 'abada _____

    and in Arabic:

    عَبَدَ _____

3. We know this word from many people's names. It has the meaning of 'servant' or 'slave' or 'worshipper.' A person who worships Allah ﷻ serves Allah ﷻ and is His slave, he or she does just what Allah ﷻ wants. Our names often show this. Some of the names that come from **'abada** are **'Abdullah** and **'Abdulatif.** Can you think of some more? **Write them on the lines below.** (Remember that often the spellings of names get changed as people move from country to country or change languages, but the sound **'abd** عَبَد will always be there at the beginning.)

_____ _____ _____

_____ _____ _____

_____ _____ _____

_____ _____ _____

4. Look at the vocabulary list for the *sūrah*. Try to find all the words that come from *'abada,* 'to worship or to serve.' Some of them will have different beginnings or endings, but all will have 'abd in some form. Write them here:

1. _____   5. _____

2. _____   6. _____

3. _____   7. _____

4. _____   8. _____

5. Another root or base word in Arabic is *ka -fa- ra*. It means to cover up, to deny. From it we get *kāfir*, a person who covers up the Truth. The plural of *kāfir* is *kāfirūn*, or *kuffār*, people who cover up the Truth. We say they cover it up because Allah ﷻ taught it to everyone in the beginning. Can you think of some other times when we cover things up? Follow the example, and write them in the space below.

we cover our bed with a bedspread
_____
_____
_____
_____

6. "For you is your *dīn* (religion) and for me is my *dīn* (religion)." Find this in your lesson and write below its transliteration (English sound):
_____

7. Can you find the verse in this *sūrah* that is repeated twice? Write it here:
_____

8. Use a mirror to read this message. Write it out on the space provided:

| la-kum dīnu-kum wa li-ya-dīn |

_____

The Abundance

Answer the following questions. Follow any given instructions:

1. *Kawthar* means a lot of or plenty of the good things of life. Of course the *kuffār* believe that life is only here on earth. For them, good things mean many children, and lots of money or land or houses.
Kawthar means something more to the Muslims. It means good and plenty in this life but especially in the next life. What are some of the good things we hope for in the life after death?

   _____   _____

   _____   _____

   _____   _____

2. Can you imagine a beautiful spring or river, full of life, all around it a very lovely land, and the water the best water in the whole universe? Can you draw what you imagine?

   The real *Kawthar* will be much better than anything we can imagine!

3. Vocabulary. Give the English definition on the blank provided:

A.   هُوَ   *huwa*   _____

B.   فَصَلّ   *Fa-Ṣalli*   _____

C.   لِ   *li*   _____

D.   إِنَّ   *'innā*   _____

E.   ٱلْأَبْتَرْ   *al-abtar*   _____

F.   رَبِّكَ   *Rabbi-ka*   _____

4. 'Sacrifice' is a big word. Allah ﷻ asked sacrifice of the Prophet ﷺ and He asks it of us.

Sacrifice can mean giving up something you love, like giving up buying sweets for a week, or giving up the money to buy a sheep. We do this in order to give the money, the sweets or the meat as *sadaqah*. We also do it to learn to control our own greed. Sacrifice can also mean giving up something bad if Allah ﷻ wants to give you something better. A person might have to give up drinking beer in order to have the water of *Al-Kawthar!* A person might have to give up some TV time, play or work time in order to have time for *ṣalāh*.

We can sacrifice many things: time, food, sleep, play, money, even friendship if Allah ﷻ asks this of us. Can you think of a few things you have sacrificed or could sacrifice for Allah ﷻ? _____

_____

_____

_____

5. When we send peace and blessings to the Prophet, *Salla-Llāhu 'alai-hi wa-Sallam,* we are keeping our connection. We are keeping ourselves from being cut off. The *kuffār* are cut off, covered up; they are on the path that leads to Allah's 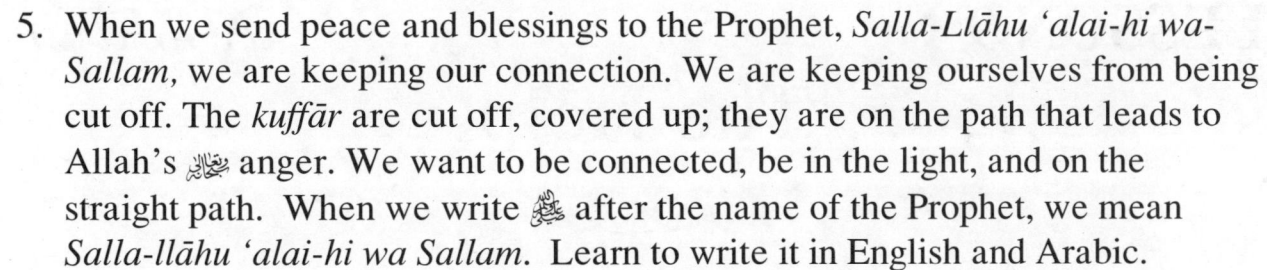 anger. We want to be connected, be in the light, and on the straight path. When we write ﷺ after the name of the Prophet, we mean *Salla-llāhu 'alai-hi wa Sallam.* Learn to write it in English and Arabic.

Ṣalla-llāhu 'alai-hi wa-Sallam

صَلَّى ٱللَّهُ عَلَيْهِ وَسَلَّم

LESSON 9

Al-Māʻūn

The Help

Answer the following questions. Follow any given directions:

1. Read the lesson and write down the characteristics of those people who "deny religion."

   A. They _____ the orphans.

   B. They _____ the needy.

   C. They _____ ṣalāh.

   D. They _____ small kindness.

   E. They do not _____ in worship.

2. Now think of the qualities of people who accept and believe in religion and complete the following sentences.

   A. They _____ the orphans.

   B. They _____ the needy.

   C. They _____ ṣalāh.

   D. They _____ small kindness.

   E. They do not _____ in worship.

3. The Prophet ﷺ said that even a smile is a gift to people. We can do a lot of small kindnesses in a day or a week. Write some of the small things you can do that are kind:

help the mother _____   _____

_____   _____

_____   _____

Illustrate one of them:

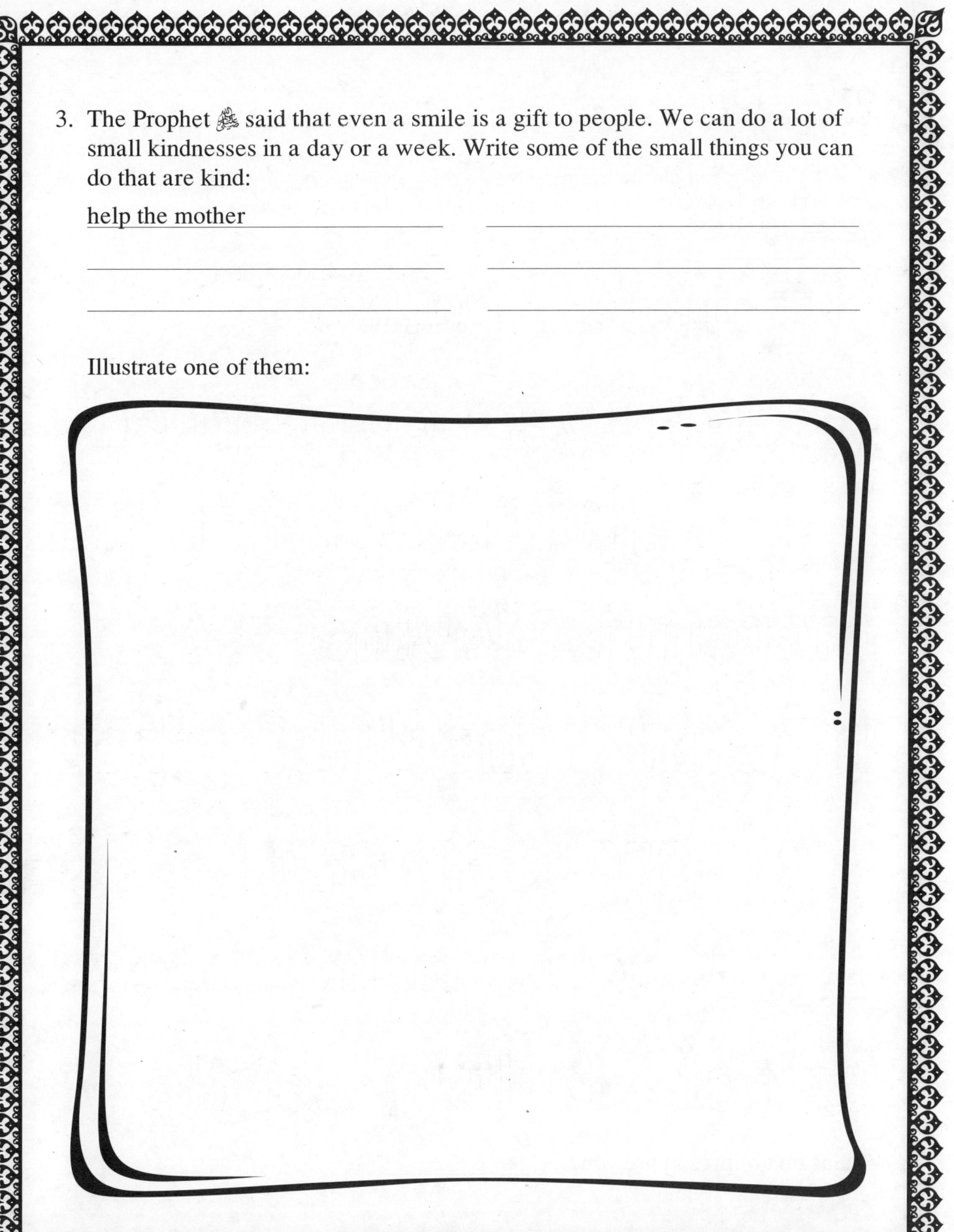

Color some of the words that describe a kind person:

caring   thoughtless

mean   polite

sensitive   concerned

selfish   thoughtful

merciful   loving

hateful   unselfish   bad

generous   mean

understanding   good

sweet   bully   gentle

What sort of person are you? _____

Answer the following questions. Follow any given instructions:

1. What are some of the ways a person could 'show off' in his or her *Ṣalāh?*

   <u>pretend to be very serious</u>

   _____

   _____

   _____

   _____

2. List the following under one of the two columns:

	ACTION OF A REAL BELIEVER	ACTION OF ONE WHO DENIES
praying from the heart (**example**)	✔	
praying to show off		
remembering the *Ṣalāh* in time		
stopping to help someone		
hurrying past everybody		
having a sour face		
sharing his or her food		
greedy for his or her own food		
always taking the best piece of cake		
giving away things he or she loves		
making you want to do good things		
never encouraging you to do good		

SMALL KINDNESS GAME

You can play this with several people or just by yourself. Use buttons or any small objects as markers. Roll dice to see how many steps you should take.

THE OBJECT OF THE GAME: You must earn 100 points to win. To do that, you count all the points you get for each kind act, and multiply by ten. You must subtract the points you lose for each unkind act, but you don't need to multiply. Why? Because Allah ﷻ is very Merciful. He gives you ten blessings for a kind act but only one sin for a bad act.

START HERE	visit sick	give *zakat*	call bad names	plant a tree	serve parents	respect adults	feed the birds	push	YOUR LUCK! ADD 5 POINTS
YOU WIN!!									read to the blind
steal									bite
pray									greet
shelter the homeless									smile
lie									share food
disrespect parents									step out of line
feed the hungry									share money
nurse the sick		Draw a picture of one act of small kindness here, in the middle of the board.							show the way
YOUR LUCK! GO UP 8 SPACES!	teach	be respectful	hit & slap	water plants	throw out trash	keep clean	take care of weak	don't do homework	SORRY! MINUS 3 POINTS

Quraish

Answer the following questions. Follow any given instructions:

1. What kinds of animals carried the goods of the Quraish?
    _____ and _____ and _____

    Draw these animals here:

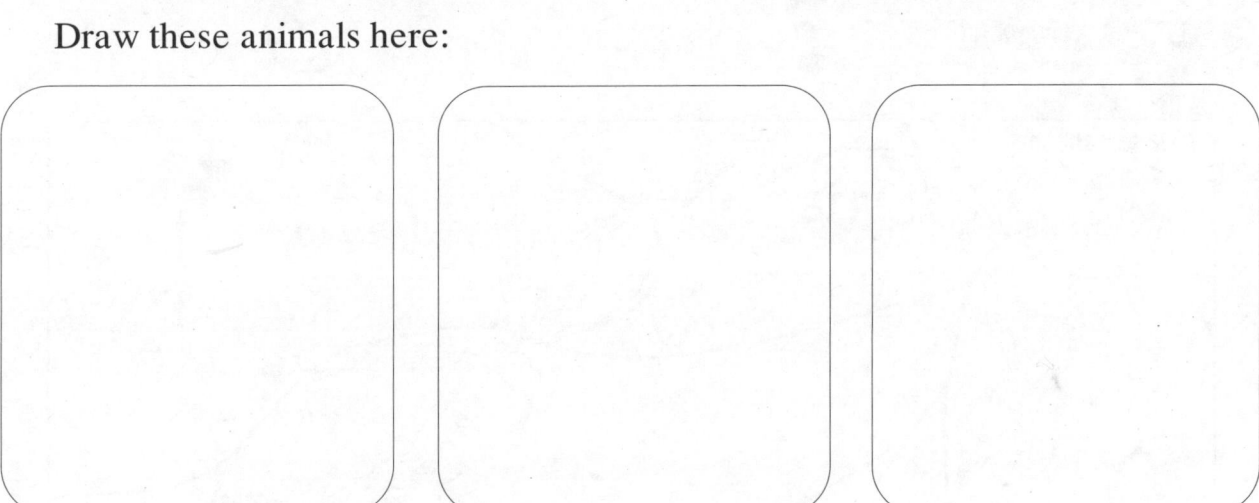

2. Draw lines between the parts of these verses of the *sūrah*. Follow the example given in letter A:

    A. In the Name of Allah   against hunger,

    B. For the covenants   from fear.

    C. Their covenants for   Most-Kind, Most-Merciful.

    D. Let them worship   the Lord of this House.

    E. Who gave them food   journeys by winter and summer.

    F. And made them secure   of the Quraish.

Map Exercise:

Here is a map of Arabia that shows the caravan routes of the Quraish. You can draw on the map some of the dangers they faced which they overcame with the help of Allah ﷻ and His protection.

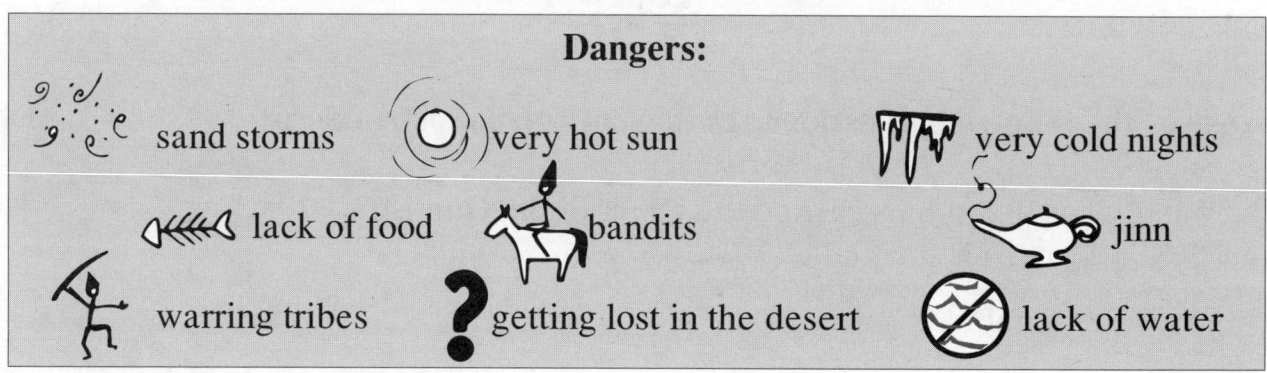

Dangers:

sand storms   very hot sun   very cold nights

lack of food   bandits   jinn

warring tribes   ? getting lost in the desert   lack of water

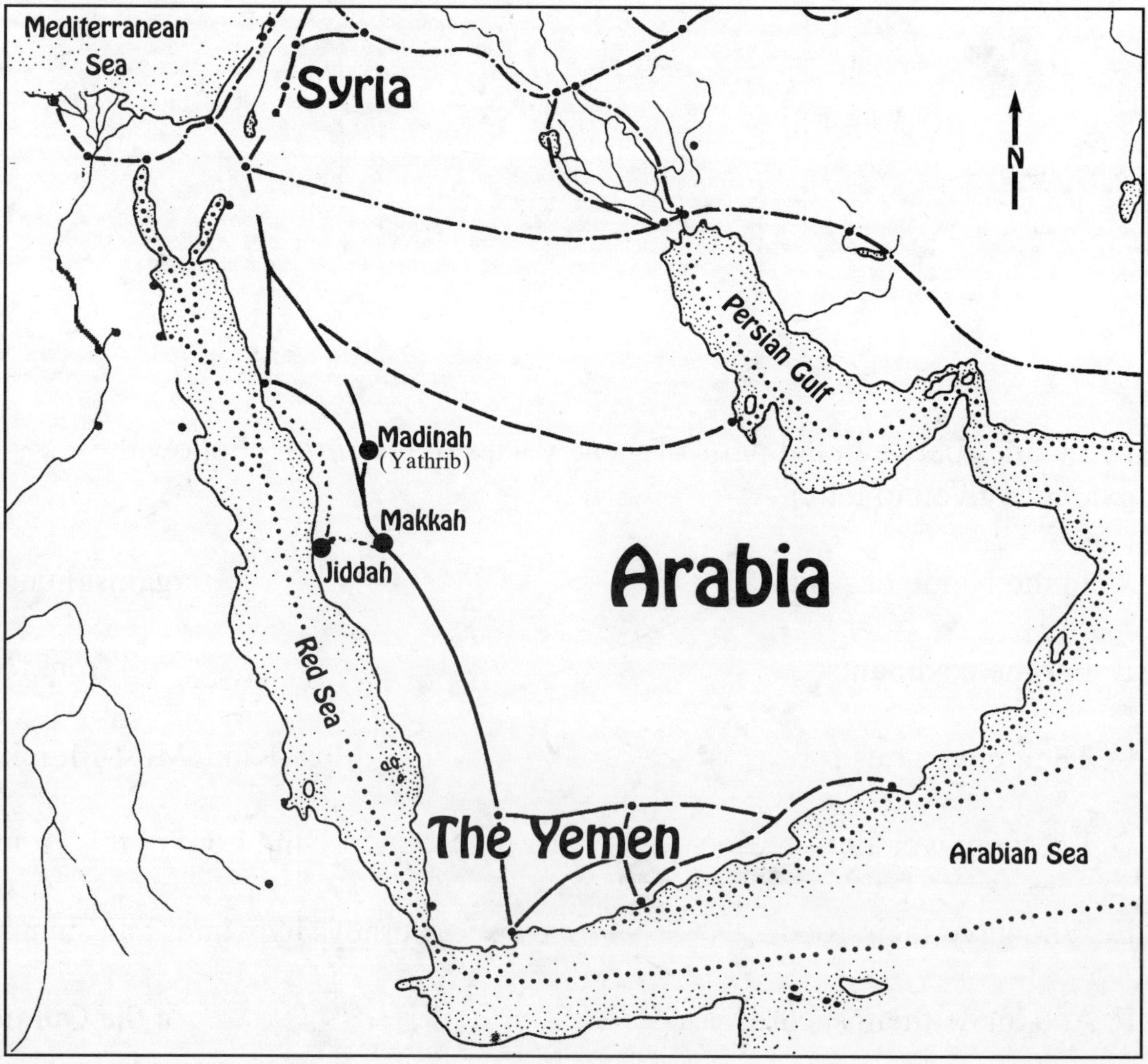

Mediterranean Sea

Syria

N

Persian Gulf

Madinah (Yathrib)

Makkah

Jiddah

Red Sea

Arabia

The Yemen

Arabian Sea

Answer the following questions. Follow any given instructions:

1. Complete the vocabulary list below:

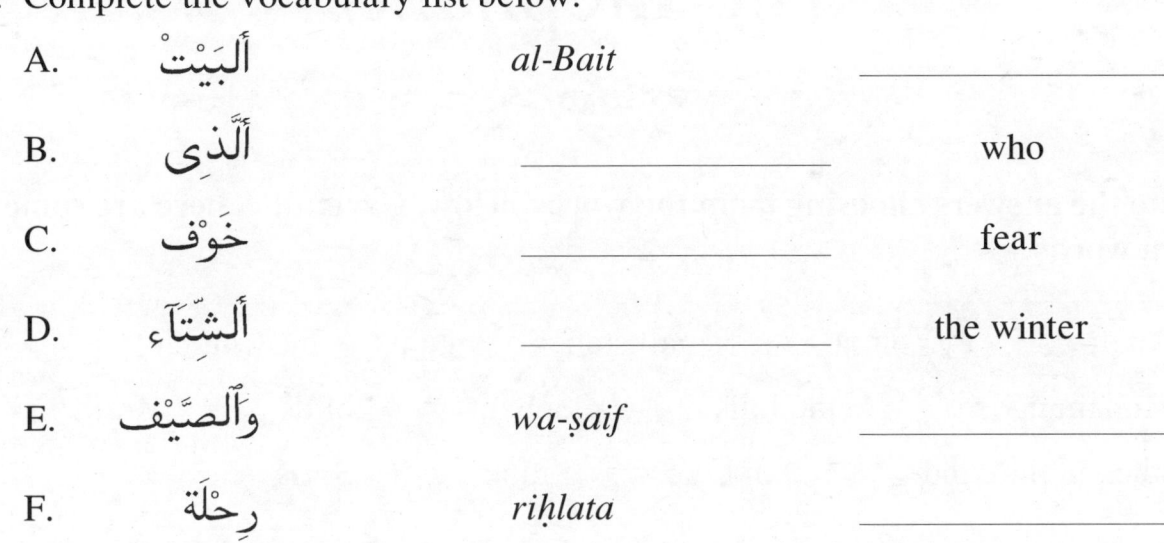

A.   أَلْبَيْتْ   *al-Bait*   _____

B.   أَلَّذِى   _____   who

C.   خَوْفٌ   _____   fear

D.   أَلشَّتَآءِ   _____   the winter

E.   وَٱلصَّيْفِ   *wa-ṣaif*   _____

F.   رِحْلَة   *riḥlata*   _____

G.   فَلْيَعْبُدُوا   *fa-lya'budū*   _____

                                                                  (review)

2. Many people say this *sūrah* when they go on a journey, even across town. Can you think of some of the troubles or dangers you need protection from when you walk or drive in your city?

a car could bump into our car _____

_____

_____

_____

_____

LESSON 11

The Elephant

Write the answers choosing from the words below. Careful! There are some extra words.

Allah ﷻ	Yemen	small stones	guns	his Church
Muhammad ﷺ	the hills	elephant	birds	afraid
stuck in the sand	Allah ﷻ	idols	Syria	

1. This *surah* tells of how Allah ﷻ defeated a very large power with some very small creatures. What are they? _____

2. What did these small creatures carry? _____

3. Abraha's country in the south was named: _____

4. Who was born in the Year of the Elephant? _____

5. Where did the Makkans hide to watch Abraha's army? _____

6. What animal was leading the army? _____

7. How did the Arabs feel about that animal? _____

8. What happened to its feet? _____

9. Who did the Quraish call the owner of the *Ka'bah?* _____

10. Who did they ask to save the *Ka'bah?* _____

11. Where did Abraha want the people to make *Ḥajj?* _____

12. Can you make a picture of what happened?

Describe your picture in your own words: _____

_____

_____

_____

Answer the following questions. Follow any given instructions:

1. There are many *surahs* that mention punishment for the enemies of Islam. Which *surahs* in this book mention Allah's ﷻ anger or punishment?

   A. _____   D. _____

   B. _____   E. _____

   C. _____

2. Which *surah* describes Allah's ﷻ nature to us? _____

3. There are many stories of something small that is stronger than something big. Remember the story of the mouse who is able to save the lion's life? Remember the story of the Prophet Dāwūd ﷺ who killed the giant Jalūt when he was only a shepherd boy? The Prophet Muhammad ﷺ also overcame something very large – the wrong beliefs of his whole family, his tribe of *Quraish,* his country of Arabia, and his whole world. You have studied 11 short *surahs* in this book. Many of them mention overcoming something difficult, or getting help and protection from something dangerous. Connect with a line the names of the *surahs* with the subjects on the right.

Name of *Surah*	Subject in the *surah*
Quraish	punishment for unkind fake Muslims
An-Nās	protection of the Ka'bah from an army
Al-Fīl	protection of Allah ﷻ from evil whisperers
Al-Falaq	punishment for a bad man
Al-Kawthar	promise of victory for the Muslims
Al-Lahab	protection of Allah ﷻ from magicians
An-Naṣr	protection of Allah ﷻ for the Quraish
Al-Mā'ūn	enemies of the Prophet ﷺ will be cut off

4. Which *sūrahs* tell us to praise, offer prayer, worship and thank Allah ﷻ?

A. _____   C. _____

B. _____   D. _____

G. Which *sūrah* says: "to you your *dīn* and to me, mine?" _____

LESSON 12 *Al-Humazah*
The Scandal-Monger / The Traducer

1. **Read the following statements, and decided whether the sentences following each statement are 'true' or 'false'.**

Statement 1

> Backbiting is not allowed for the Muslims.
> It is a bad habit. Rasulullah ﷺ said,
> "Say Something nice, or keep quiet."

a. Karim talks bad things about some of his friends when they are not there. He also thinks he is good Muslim and he follows Rasulullah ﷺ.

   Karim is: ◯ RIGHT   ◯ WRONG

b. Salma tries to follow the *Hadith,* She never talks bad things about any one. Salma does not like to backbite.

   Salma follows Rasulullah ﷺ: ◯ TRUE   ◯ FALSE

Statement 2

> Both, *Humazah* and *Lumazah* believe that
> their good fortune in this world would save
> them from the accounting in the *Akhirah*.
> They think that their family and money would
> last for ever, however, they are wrong as this
> is not going to happen.

a. Laila's parents have lot money. Laila always Follows the Sunnah and never backbites or hurt any one. She believes that Allah ﷻ will reward her good actions.

Laila is: ◯ Right   ◯ Wrong

2. **Read *Surah Al-Humazah* and sequence the following verses in the order in which they are given in the *Surah*.**

◯ يَحْسَبُ أَنَّ مَالَهُۥٓ أَخْلَدَهُۥ

◯ وَيْلٌ لِّكُلِّ هُمَزَةٍ لُّمَزَةٍ

◯ كَلَّا لَيُنۢبَذَنَّ فِى ٱلْحُطَمَةِ

◯ نَارُ ٱللَّهِ ٱلْمُوقَدَةُ

◯ فِى عَمَدٍ مُّمَدَّدَةٍ

◯ ٱلَّتِى تَطَّلِعُ عَلَى ٱلْأَفْـِٔدَةِ

◯ وَمَآ أَدْرَىٰكَ مَا ٱلْحُطَمَةُ

◯ إِنَّهَا عَلَيْهِم مُّؤْصَدَةٌ

◯ ٱلَّذِى جَمَعَ مَالًا وَعَدَّدَهُۥ

3. VOCABULARY

Connect the following words with their meanings with a line.

كُلِّ

هُمَزَةٍ

لُّمَزَةٍ

مَالاً

ٱلَّذِى

مَالاً

وَعَدَّدَهُ

كَلَّا

فِى

ٱلْحُطَمَةُ

نَارُ

ٱلْمُوقَدَةُ

تَطَّلِعُ

ٱلْأَفْئِدَةِ

Kulli	every
Humazatin	who
Lumazah	slanderer
Malan	backbiter
'Alladhi	gathered
Jama'a	money
Wa 'addadah	into
Kalla	and counted it
Fi	certainly not
'al-hutmah	the fire of
Naru	the crusher
'al-muqadah	jumps up
tattali'u	the hearts
'al-af idah	lit

LESSON 13

The Time/The Decling Day

1.   Think, and write down two things (in each category) which you will do.

Statement 1

"We have to use our time wisely."

CATEGORIES

Read   Pray   Help

Share   Listen   Watch

Do   Talk

Statement 2

We should not waste our time

CATEGORIES

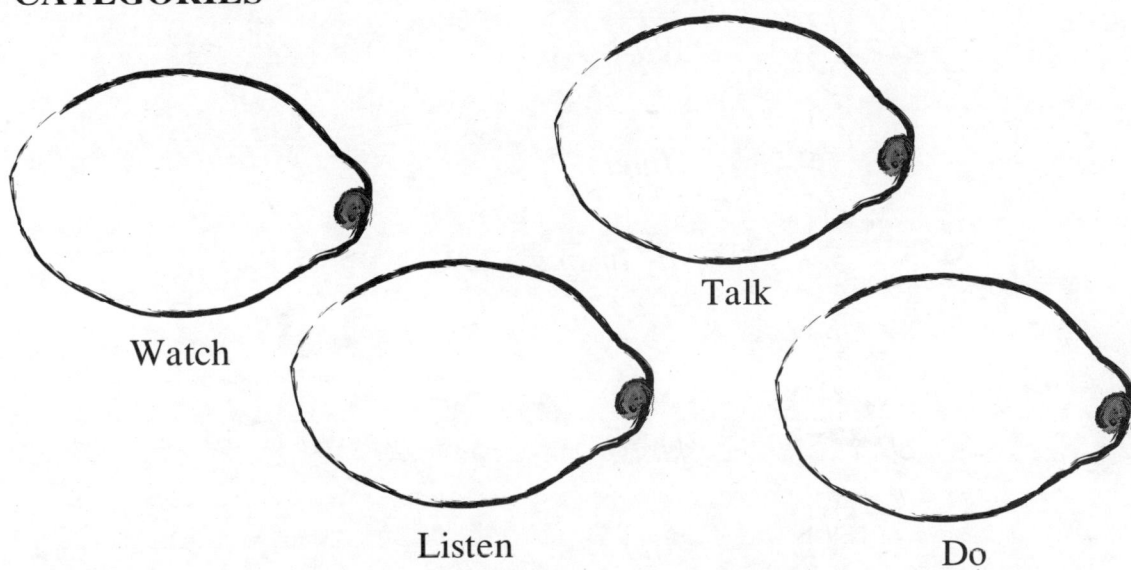

Watch

Talk

Listen

Do

2. write the story of the ice seller in your own words.

    _____

    _____

    _____

    _____

3. write the good habits of those people who are NOT at a loss as Allah ﷻ
    tells us in *Ayah* 3 of *Surah Al 'Asr.*

    a. _____

    b. _____

    c. _____

    d. _____

4. VOCABULARY

Learn the meanings of the Arabic words then write them down below.

Arabic words	transliteration	Meanings
وَٱلْعَصْرِ	Wa-l-'Aṣr	_____
إِنَّ	'Inna	_____
ٱلْإِنسَـٰنَ	al-'Insāna	_____
لَفِى	la-fī	_____
خُسْرٍ	khusr	_____
إِلَّا	'Illa	_____
ٱلَّذِينَ	Alladhīna	_____
ءَامَنُواْ	'Āmanū	_____
وَعَمِلُواْ	wa-'amilū	_____
ٱلصَّـٰلِحَـٰتِ	as-ṣāliḥati	_____
وَتَوَاصَوْاْ	wa-tawāṣaw	_____
بِٱلْحَقِّ	bi-l-ḥaqqi	_____
وَتَوَاصَوْاْ	wa-tawāṣaw	_____
بِٱلصَّبْرِ	bi-ṣ-ṣabri	_____

LESSON 14   *At-Takathur*
Piling up / Rivalry in Worldly Increase

1. **Circle the possible reason for the following actions of some people.**

ACTION: They are always working to collect more and more money.

    POSSIBLE REASON:

        Want to have a lot of wealth.

        Want to help others.

        Think of Allah ﷻ all the time.

ACTION: They always share with others whatever Allah ﷻ has given them.

    POSSIBLE REASON:

        Want to be rich.

        Want to follow Allah's command and help others.

        Think only about their comfort.

ACTION: Believers are thankful to Allah ﷻ, whether they get more or less.

   POSSIBLE REASON:

   They are lazy.

   They do not care.

   They have *Qana'ah* (contentment).

2. **Think of the things which usually people think will make them happy. List only three of them below.**

   a. _____

   b. _____

   c. _____

3. **Following *Ayah of Surah At-Takathur* have been placed in a mixed order. Number them in the correct order.**

   ⬡ كَلَّا سَوْفَ تَعْلَمُونَ

   ⬡ لَتَرَوُنَّ ٱلْجَحِيمَ

   ⬡ ثُمَّ كَلَّا سَوْفَ تَعْلَمُونَ

   ⬡ ثُمَّ لَتَرَوُنَّهَا عَيْنَ ٱلْيَقِينِ

   ⬡ حَتَّىٰ زُرْتُمُ ٱلْمَقَابِرَ

   ⬡ كَلَّا لَوْ تَعْلَمُونَ عِلْمَ ٱلْيَقِينِ

   ⬡ أَلْهَىٰكُمُ ٱلتَّكَاثُرُ

   ⬡ ثُمَّ لَتُسْـَٔلُنَّ يَوْمَئِذٍ عَنِ ٱلنَّعِيمِ

4. VOCABULARY

Write the Arabic word(S) for each English word or phrase.

ENGLISH	ARABIC
Distracts you	_____
Competition in	_____
Worldly increase	_____
Until	_____
You visit	_____
The graves	_____
But no	_____
(soon) you will know	_____
And then, again but no	_____
But no, if	_____
You will know	_____
Knowledge of certainty	_____
You shall certainly see	_____
Hell-fire	_____
But again	_____
Sight of certainty, sure	_____
You shall be surely asked	_____
On that day	_____
About the joy	_____

Dear Students!

Switch your work with your friend and check each other's work to make sure that you have got it.

May Allah, Most High, bless you and guide your studies and your *dīn.*
❦   *AMĪN*   ❧

بِسْمِ اللَّهِ الرَّحْمَنِ الرَّحِيمِ

إِنَّمَا نُطْعِمُكُمْ لِوَجْهِ اللَّهِ لَا نُرِيدُ مِنكُمْ
جَزَاءً وَلَا شُكُورًا ﴿٩﴾

We feed you only for the countenance of Allah. We wish not from you reward or gratitude.

(The Holy Qur'an, 76:9)

IQRA' wishes to thank  Zakat Foundation for their contribution to the printing of this book. Please visit the Zakat Foundation of America at **www.zakat.org** to support their many noble and much needed causes.